Old GARELOCHHEAD &
the ROSNEATH PENINSULA

by
Keith Hall

Row, from Gareloch.

By the 1890s, Rosneath's wooden pier, which had stood since 1845, had fallen into disrepair and the Duke of Argyll decided it would be cheaper to build a new one (pictured). This opened in 1893 and the wood from its predecessor provided the fuel for a bonfire on Rosneath Point to celebrate the marriage of the Duke of York that same year. On the outbreak of the Second World War, the pier was closed to civilian use due to the military presence in the area; the US Army had a large base that covered most of the area now occupied by the newer houses in the village. The pier was closed to all use in 1942 although its remains can still be seen just south of the Ferry Inn.

© Keith Hall, 1999
First published in the United Kingdom, 1999,
by Stenlake Publishing,
Ochiltree Sawmill, The Lade,
Ochiltree, Ayrshire, KA18 2NX
Telephone / Fax: 01290 423114

ISBN 1 84033 060 0

FOREWORD

This book makes no pretensions of being a definitive history – the books listed in the bibliography provide a far more comprehensive and in-depth overview of the area's past. Instead, it is intended as a window to the past. In the foreword to F.M. Crum's *The Isle of Rosneath*, Dr Warr wrote, 'I was transported back to the peaceful and remote Rosneath in which I spent my happy childhood half a century ago, when there were no buses and no motor cars, and when the steamer and the ferryman were the only links with the outside world.' If this small book in any way captures that sentiment, then it achieves its purpose.

Many of the photographs featured come from private collections and most have not been published before; so apart from enjoying the book and stirring memories, I hope it might encourage some readers to delve into their own old pictures and share them, for they are now the 'keepers of the past'. The Local History section of the library is a good and welcoming home for these pictures or at least copies of them.

This Garelochhead church was built by 'immigrants' from the east coast in 1873. It became the United Free in 1900 and combined with the parish church in 1938. During the war the building served as a canteen and later it was used for dances and as the lodge of the local Royal Arch Chapter of Freemasons before demolition in the 1970s. Behind is the Gibson Hall, erected in 1898 and now the community centre.

Garelochhead from the Station.

One of the earliest records of Garelochhead is Timothy Pont's map of 1654 which shows a small village at the loch head called Kean Loch Gherr ('head of the short loch'). The history of the village is sparse and it has tended to be overshadowed by the parishes of Rosneath and Rhu on either side of it (both of which were prominent in ecclesiastical circles at various times). Until 1838 people from Garelochhead, Strone or Finnart had to travel the eight or nine miles to the parish church at Row (the spelling was changed to the original Gaelic – Rhu – in 1927) but to remedy this a second church for the parish, known as a 'chapel of ease', was built (pictured in the centre background) and is still in use today.

Steamer at Garelochhead Pier.

The first pier at Garelochhead was built in 1845 and was the scene of the infamous 'Battle of Garelochhead Pier' one Sunday in August, 1853. The local laird, James Colquhoun, disapproved of Sunday sailings and with the help of some local people, barricaded the pier in an attempt to prevent the P.S. *Emperor* from berthing. However, the laird lost the day after a determined challenge from the steamer's crew. By the 1850s six different steamers called at the pier and a new one, pictured, was built in 1879. Its predecessor was demolished in 1881.

4

The pier, 1934. The popularity of steamer services along the Clyde and beyond, beginning with the *Comet* in 1812, was quickly established and going 'doon the watter' on a day trip became a regular pastime for most of the working class of Glasgow. Towns along the routes developed facilities to take advantage of this new passing trade and, although initially the most popular destinations were well-established towns such as Rothesay, Dunoon, Largs and Ayr, the villages on the Gare Loch soon became big attractions as well.

The Garelochhead Hotel first opened its doors in the 1850s to take advantage of this new trade, although the steamers themselves provided plenty of liquid refreshment for the passengers and many effectively became floating pubs. The hotel remained in business until 1992 and, abandoned and left to the vandals, it was eventually demolished a few years later.

The Anchor Inn was built on the site of a house that was destroyed in the 1830s. The steamer services improved communications between the Gare Loch and Glasgow and the area soon became a much favoured site for the residences of the city's professional and business people. Although by the 1860s the railway network was spreading out from Glasgow up the Dunbartonshire coast to Craigendoran, the railway was not to take advantage of this trade further up the coast for another three decades.

Long before the introduction of the steamers, the Loch was recognised as a shelter for naval vessels. It was frequently a station of the Scottish royal navies and during the Napoleonic Wars ships of the Royal Navy were also based there. Military use of the loch was stepped up in the twentieth century and it was used to test many of the naval vessels that had been built on the Clyde. One of these was the K13, a steam powered submarine which sank off Shandon in 1917 on her voyage from Fairfields Yard at Govan. She was submerged for two days and of the eighty men on board, thirty died. During the Second World War the whole area was practically taken over for military use with the military port at Faslane and its associated camps at Stuckenduff and Blairvadock. After the war the Faslane base was used as a ship breaking yard and in 1958 the Royal Navy 'moved in' when they harboured their submarine depot ship H.M.S. *Adamant* there.

As well as the steamers and the railways, the 1920s also saw the development of another public transport – buses and charabancs. The bus operator in Garelochhead was Henry Brown's Motor Services and two of his vehicles are pictured here outside the Post Office in 1924.

Station Road, Garelochhead.

When it was constructed in the 1890s, the West Highland Line had to be built on the hill above the loch. The railway's proprietors hoped that the new service would lure passengers away from the ferries, but unfortunately the approaches to the stations were long and steep – a situation which led to complaints. A disgruntled passenger wrote to the *Railway Herald*: 'Sound heart and lungs and experience in hill climbing are essential to a man who hurries from the breakfast table to catch a train at one of the lochside stations. It is easier to go to the pier.'

Oxford Place around the turn of the century.

The Shore Road looking south, 1946.

Another area of the village that has more or less remained unchanged is Whistlefield Brae, pictured here at the turn of the century.

The smiddy at Garelochhead was just off Whistlefield Brae. It was situated down the now private road known as Smiddy Lane.

The tramp steamer S.S. *Siberian* pictured after she was blown from her moorings in the Gare Loch during a gale in January 1919. This was not the first accident the ship was involved in. In December 1910, during a severe snowstorm, she dragged her anchor into the path of the steamer *Lucy Ashton*. In the collision the steamer's bows were stove in, but she managed to struggle back to her base at Craigendoran. Luckily, only two passengers were injured.

The Gare Loch, 1931. On several occasions the loch was used as a 'ship park', for example during the recession of the 1930s when sufficient cargoes for ships could not be found. Again, after the Second World War, the loch was used to store the reserve fleet (ships used in the war which were no longer required in peacetime) prior to its disposal.

A view of the Gare Loch and the Wayside Tearoom from Whistlefield, 1939. The circular structure in the foreground is the water tank that supplied water to the tearoom and the surrounding houses.

RAILWAY STATION, WHISTLEFIELD, LOCH LONG.

93688.JE

Under the terms of the 1889 West Highland Railway Act, the North British Railway Company undertook to build a station at Portincaple and also intended to implement a ferry service from the hamlet to Loch Goil. However, despite objections from the locals, the station was never built. Eventually, the station at Whistlefield (pictured here in 1924) was opened in 1896 and remained in use until 1964 when it was closed along with the other lochside stations at Rhu, Shandon and Glen Douglas.

Inn Restaurant, Whistlefield.

This tearoom took advantage of trade from day-trippers. Whistlefield was at one time on the old drover's trail from Argyll. Cattle were ferried across Loch Long to Portincaple and from there driven to the markets in Glasgow. The drovers tended to keep to the high ground above the lochside villages so that they could avoid paying tolls.

The Whistlefield Inn served as a resting place for travellers, usually from Glasgow, who were passengers on the popular ferry and rail tours through the region.

The Peddison family, holidaymakers from England, pictured outside the Inn in the 1950s.

A few miles north of Garelochhead, standing on the banks of Loch Long, is Portincaple. Although it was not served by a pier, the Arrocher steamer was known to stop by the hamlet and land passengers by boat. Between 1897 and 1906, it was the landing place for the 'Circular Tour', a ferry trip which took tourists around Loch Long, the Gare Loch and Loch Lomond before they went on to catch the train to Glasgow at Whistlefield.

Portincaple, (Loch Long.)

4056/6

Portincaple was a small fishing community, although the arrival of the steamers and, later, the trains encouraged some people to build homes there.

CLYNDER ROAD, RAHANE

220/37

Rahane in the 1920s, the first settlement on the coastal road around the peninsula. The main occupation on the peninsula was fishing and in the early 1800s there were 43 fishing boats based on it, crewed by around 120 local men. Slate was also once quarried above Clynder but the operation soon proved uneconomical and was abandoned in the early 1900s.

Clynder Hotel, pictured on the left in 1957, was destroyed by fire in the early 1990s. The hamlet's first pier was built in 1886 but was soon superseded by another pier further to the north built by the Robert Thom, the owner of the Barreman Estate. He probably wanted to attract potential feuars and his pier boasted a crane and a large waiting room. There was some local opposition to the new pier and although it was only 500 yards away from the old one, the somewhat ludicrous situation occurred where steamers called at them both. However, Thom's pier gradually won the lion's share of passengers as it was better built and had safer approaches than its southern rival which gradually fell into disrepair and was demolished in 1893. Thom's pier, on the other hand, survived until 1942 when steamer services ceased due to military use of the loch.

The U.P. church and manse (now a gallery) at Clynder. The church was built in 1881 and was constructed from corrugated metal. Later, it was dismantled by the McGruers and rebuilt at Hattonburn where they used it as the premises of their canteen. The staff used to sit at the pews to have their meals. The church still stands beside the new houses at Hattonburn.

The shops and hotel at Clynder in the 1940s. Arthur Payne owned the Old Manse before moving his business to Rosneath.

The brothers Gruer and Ewing McGruer opened their first boatyard at Rutherglen in 1897 and Ewing (his brother having disappeared) bought the boat building yard – originally Tait's boatyard – at Hattonburn, Clynder, in 1910. The family caught the Clyde puffer *Urchin* to move up to the site and on arriving in the Gare Loch the skipper simply ran aground at Hattonburn to make it easy for the them to move their possessions ashore. From the 1920s to the 1970s the family did much to encourage and promote yachting in the area and they hosted the 'School's Week' for the Mudhook Yacht Club (the schoolchildren's club). The Clynder yard remained in business until 1983 when all the equipment was moved to their other yard at Rosneath. The site was then sold for housing development.

The paddle steamer *Lucy Ashton* at Rosneath pier just after the Second World War. Built by T.B. Seath & Co. of Rutherglen, she was launched in May 1888 and initially operated on the North British Railway Company's Holy Loch route. In common with their other steamers, all of which were based at Craigendoran, she bore the name of a character from the works of Sir Walter Scott, in this case the ill-fated heroine of *The Bride of Lammermoor* (the 'island' of Rosneath featured in *The Heart of Midlothian*). Later, she was transferred to the Gare Loch route where she stayed until 1939 when the Craigendoran services were cut back. On the outbreak of war most of the steamer fleet was requisitioned for military use but the *Lucy Ashton* remained to ply the route south to Dunoon and, after the submarine boom was lifted in 1945, to Rothesay. Her last voyage, from Craigendoran to Dunoon, was in 1949. She was taken to Faslane for breaking up and a Glasgow firm purchased her siren. This was given to a business in Santiago, Chile, and for many years its was used to call the employees to work.

The Annual District Church Parade passing through the Clachan at Rosneath, 1959. The parish has had a church since the twelfth century and St Modan's, the present parish church, was built in 1853 to replace an earlier kirk which had stood since 1780. The name of the parish has been given various interpretations: Rhos-noeth, the 'bare or unwooded promontory'; Ros-na-choich, the 'Virgin's promontory'; and Ross-Neyt, the 'point of Neyt or Neuth', possibly the name of the first parish priest. The church contains the 1610 Bugerhuis Bell which in 1715 rang out to warn of the first Jacobite rebellion and also features the reredos of the Last Supper, carved by Meredith Williams, which was presented by Princess Louise in 1931 in memory of her husband, the 9th Duke of Argyll.

The original Ferry Inn was a thatched single-storey building situated some 400 yards south of the present building and about 1800 its replacement was built using stones from the derelict Camsail House. The Inn was then extended three times between 1862 and 1893. Princess Louise, then Marchioness of Lorne, had thoughts of living there herself (she is even said to have painted the Inn's sign which hung over the door) and around 1890 she commissioned Sir Edwin Lutyens to build the extension with three chimneys (the Inn thereafter comprised of two buildings: the old building – the pub – is pictured under the tree and was later demolished). However, she instead moved to the Clachan and later to Rosneath Castle. During the Boer War the Inn became a hostel for wounded soldiers and it was requisitioned by the government for military use in 1939. After the war it was used as married quarters until 1958.

The first castle at Rosneath was known as Easter House and although the date of its construction is unknown it was converted by the Argylls in 1630 into a subsidiary residence to their castle at Inverary. It was situated on the lochside at Castle Bay but was destroyed by fire in 1802. The Duke replaced it with this mansion, designed by Joseph Bonomi – whose Italian origins are evident in the final design – and built between 1803 and 1805. The house was sold on the death of Princess Louise in 1939 and was then used as the headquarters for the American forces based in Rosneath during the war. It was abandoned after the war and eventually demolished in 1961.

The Old Corn Mill, Rosneath, Gareloch.

The parish entry of the Statistical Account of 1799 recounts the strange nature of the peninsula's soil. Apparently, it was famed for its fatality to rats: 'Here rats cannot exist. Many of these have, at different times, been accidentally imported from vessels lying upon the shore, but were never known to live twelve months in the place. From a prevailing opinion, that the soil of this parish is hostile to that animal, some years ago a West India planter actually carried out to Jamaica several casks of Rosneath earth, with a view to killing the rats that were destroying his sugar canes. It is said this had not the desired effect, so we lost a very valuable export. Had the experiment succeeded, this would have been a new and profitable trade for the proprietors, but perhaps by this time the parish of Rosneath might have been no more.' Referring to this story, accounts of the area from the nineteenth century were quick to point out that rats had since got over their aversion to the peninsula, but probably this was due to corn mills such as this springing up to feed the population.

Rosneath's first boatyard was opened in 1867 by Archibald McKellar, who later also opened the yard at Kilcreggan known as 'McKellar's Slipway'. In 1891 the Rosneath yard was bought by Peter McLean who soon sold it on so that he could concentrate on another of his acquisitions, the Clynder Hotel. By 1909, one of the apprentices at the yard, James Silver (whose father was then the local grocer and baker), already having secured commissions of his own, was ready to set up a business himself. That year the then owner committed suicide and Silver joined forces with John McCallum, a well known yacht designer, to buy the yard. It is pictured here just after they bought it. Silver established himself as a builder of fine yachts but unfortunately by keeping his prices low, the yard ran up debts and by 1914 the business went into voluntary liquidation.

The yard was taken over by Ferguson & Thompson Ltd of Glasgow, a chandlers and brokerage firm, who kept on the Silver name and for a while, as manager, the man himself. In 1916 Silver was replaced by John Bain and the yard prospered under this temperamental workaholic. By the mid-1930s, about a hundred people were employed there and the management even built the flats known as 'Silverhills' to house them. Bain's nickname amongst the workforce was 'Hurricane Jack of the Vital Spark' and it was said that they could tell what sort of day they were going to have by the speed at which he walked into the yard in the morning. Pictured in 1965, the yachts under construction at the yard are, from left to right, the *Silver Buccaneer*, the *Mamora*, the *Silver Sula* and the *Mary Fisher*.

A launching at the yard in the 1920s. By the fifties, Bain (the man in the cap on the right) was a major shareholder in the yard but in 1957 it was taken over by other shareholders, John Boyd and Peter Boyle. Although he was offered a directorship, Bain preferred to become their freelance designer and after parting company with the yard worked for another yacht builder in Fife. He was still designing yachts well into his eighties and died in 1980, aged 91. Silvers was wound up in 1971 and since then the yard has changed hands several times. The present owners, however, are keeping memories alive by naming their company Silvers Marine Ltd.

A 28 foot cabin launch built by the yard during the early 1920s. In the background is the Clyde Training Ship *Empress*, an ex-Royal Navy warship which was effectively a floating reform school that catered for up to 400 boys. The ship was paid for by several leading Glasgow businessmen and it replaced the *Cumberland* which they had moved to the Gareloch for this purpose in 1879. This first ship lasted until 1889 when, allegedly, she was set alight by some of the boys.

Kilcreggan, 1921. Originally a mere cluster of small farms and cottages linked by ferry to the Ferry Inn at Rosneath, the development of the village after the start of the steamer services was much more impressive than elsewhere on the peninsula as it was very close to Greenock by ferry. The initial feus were taken up on the Shore Road in the 1880s and later, when more land was required, a road higher up the hill was built. The tenement blocks opposite the pier were built between 1888 and 1903.

The waterfront at Kilcreggan. Over the centuries the lands of Rosneath Parish passed through the hands of many of the region's landowning families. In 1264 they were held by Alexander Duncan and then passed on to the Drummonds, ancestors of the House of Perth. They were then owned by Alexander de Monteith By the fifteenth century part of the peninsula was owned by the Earls of Lennox who dominated much of Dunbartonshire and most of the land on the east side of the loch.

KILCREGGAN

The Lennox family became prominent in national affairs in the 1400s and were involved in various political and military machinations throughout their period of dominance in Dunbartonshire. In 1425 the current Earl and other members of the family were executed at Stirling and in 1489 his successor, 'having been involved in treasonable undertakings', had his lands confiscated by the Crown. He was subsequently pardoned but his property at Rosneath remained confiscated and was given as a gift to the 1st Earl of Argyll. In more recent times the peninsula was divided into three estates: the Duke of Argyll's to the south and west; Barreman to the east; and Peatoun in the north.

From the three churches built to serve the rapidly expanding population of Kilcreggan and the surrounding area, Craigrownie Parish Church is the sole survivor. Built as a chapel of ease in 1852, it had to be enlarged in 1889. An Irish mason, John McElroy, who feued large parts of Cove was responsible for drawing up the plans. Cove Burgh Hall was built in 1893 and now is home to Cove Library.

In the early years of the steamers, there was a lot of rivalry between the various companies and there are many stories about steamers racing for the pier at Kilcreggan, built in 1850, to get their passengers off first. The pier was rebuilt in 1897 and although the steamers were eventually withdrawn at the end of the 1933 season, the buildings were renewed and the pier structure strengthened in 1964. It is the only traditional pier that remains open all year round on the Clyde and it is a stop for the *Waverley* and the Gourock ferry.

The remains of the Cove and Kilcreggan Gas works. Before 1935 the only public services provided on the peninsula were water and gas and these were only supplied to the west side of the peninsula, the police burgh of Kilcreggan and Cove. The water supply was established in 1882 and came from Lochan Glas Laoigh but the rest of the peninsula had to wait until 1937 when the pipeline from Whistlefield Reservoir, which already served Garelochhead, was extended down the eastern shore. In 1871 the Cove and Kilcreggan Gas Company was formed and had its works near the Barbour Cemetery. The coal required to produce the gas was brought in by puffers which were beached so that coal could be unloaded and 'waste' coke taken away. Electricity was brought to the peninsula in 1935 by cables laid from Rhu under the Gare Loch. By July of that year 42 houses in Rosneath and Clynder and 33 in Cove and Kilcreggan were using it.

Church Parade

Portkil Kilcreggan

T.B.F.

Soldiers of the Garrison Artillery (a territorial regiment) at a field service. They manned the Portkil Battery which was constructed at the turn of the century. The guns were never fired in anger, except when the *Vital Spark* was fired upon in one of the Para Handy books!

The military hospital at Portkil, built by the American forces in 1942. After the war the site was used as a barracks by the Royal Navy until it was demolished in the early 1950s.

With the expansion of the ferry services in the late 1840s and fifties, piers began to proliferate at many sites often before any village or habitation existed. At Cove, for example, the pier was built in 1852 by the landowners to encourage feuars and the first houses were built around the landing place.

Aside from being a grocer, draper and general merchant, William Gordon Jr also published booklets of photographs to sell to tourists and this picture of his shop at Cove is from one of them. Before sophisticated commercial operations such as his appeared, whisky smuggling was often a way for local folk to make a living in the eighteenth and early nineteenth centuries. When George IV visited Scotland in the 1830s, the area's illicit stills had reputation enough for him to express a desire to taste real smuggled whisky and the Duke of Argyll was despatched to acquire a barrel for him.

Knockderry Castle was built in 1855, supposedly on the remains of the dungeons of an ancient Norwegian or Danish lookout tower, and it was extended in 1896. It was used by the Free French as a hospital during the Second World War and this photograph was taken in the early 1960s, by which time it had become a guest house (it is now a private residence). The photograph was used as a postcard and the message on the back reads: '. . . misty just now. It's raining at the moment, but perhaps it will be dry tomorrow . . .' Some things don't change, it would appear, nor do people's aspirations!